To:

_____

From:

Endorsements

When you teach children that they can talk to Creator God and that He listens to what they say, you are setting them up for a lifetime of intimacy and communion with Him. Jesus reminds us all through Scripture that we are to come to Him as little children: full of faith, trust, and dependence upon Him. *I Can Learn to Pray* is an outstanding resource for families as, together, you learn what it means to communicate with God. Watch and see!

—Dr. Jack Graham, pastor of
Prestonwood Baptist Church

If the highest goal of Christian parents is to see their children walk with God, we couldn't have a better friend than Holly Hawkins Shivers. After the very popular *I Can Learn the Bible*, Holly is back to help us again with *I Can Learn to Pray*. Get these resources and see God use them to instill the faith in your family.

—Dr. James McDonald, senior pastor
of Harvest Bible Chapel

Prayer precedes God's power and wisdom in life. This is why every person needs to be taught how to pray, including our children and grandchildren. *I Can Learn to Pray* helps children and their parents in practical ways to learn how to talk to God. Leave your child a great legacy. Teach them how to pray.

—Dr. Ronnie Floyd, president of the
Southern Baptist Convention and
senior pastor of Cross Church, and
Jeana Floyd

Just as a team needs a game plan for playing football, we believe we need a game plan for raising our four kids to know and love God. *I Can Learn to Pray* will be part of our plan as we teach our kids just how to draw near to God. Holly takes profound truths of prayer and makes them simple for kids to understand. We highly recommend this book . . . get in the game with us!

> —Jason Witten, tight end for the
> Dallas Cowboys, and Michelle
> Witten

Holly Shivers has done it again! *I Can Learn to Pray* is the ideal follow-up to her first children's book, *I Can Learn the Bible*. Holly not only proposes that children develop a prayer habit, she also describes a plan of action that is intentional and doable. I highly recommend this book to parents, churches, and anyone in the faith community who wants to take their children to a deeper level of commitment, reverence, and love for our Lord Jesus Christ.

> —Dr. Larry Taylor, head of
> Prestonwood Christian Academy

I Can Learn to Pray

52 Devotions
on Talking to God

By Holly Hawkins Shivers

Tommy
NELSON

A Division of Thomas Nelson Publishers

I Can Learn to Pray

© 2016 Holly Hawkins Shivers

Published in Nashville, Tennessee, by Tommy Nelson. Tommy Nelson is an imprint of Thomas Nelson. Thomas Nelson is a registered trademark of HarperCollins Christian Publishing, Inc.

Illustrated by Becka Moore

Tommy Nelson titles may be purchased in bulk for educational, business, fund-raising, or sales promotional use. For information, please e-mail SpecialMarkets@ThomasNelson.com.

ISBN-13: 978-0-7180-8169-0

Library of Congress Cataloging-in-Publication Data
Shivers, Holly Hawkins, author.
I can learn to pray : 52 devotions on talking to God / by Holly Hawkins Shivers.
pages cm
Summary: "Responding to the felt need of parents who want to help their children build a close personal relationship with God, I Can Learn to Pray will show children the importance of prayer and how to pray. Holly Hawkins Shivers is leading by living as she teaches her children and others how to build a close relationship with God through prayer. Through simple examples of prayers, children not only learn the importance of prayer but also how to pray--to praise, confess, pray for others, ask for help, and express gratitude. Stories about how God works through our prayers show children the power, comfort, and love they can feel through prayer. And the practice of prayer engages kids and helps them feel comfortable and confident praying. After adapting her father O. S. Hawkins's book The Joshua Code into a kid-friendly devotional that helps children learn and live the Scriptures in I Can Learn the Bible, Shivers takes the next step in discipleship. These two books will work together as a solid foundation for both parents and kids for years to come."-- Provided by publisher.
Audience: Ages 4-8
ISBN 978-0-7180-8169-0 (hardcover)
1. Prayer--Christianity -Juvenile literature. 2. Children--Prayers and devotions. 3. Children--Religious life. 4. Christian life--Juvenile literature. I. Title.
BV212.S53 2016
242.62--dc23
2015022367

Printed in China
16 17 18 19 20 TIMS 6 5 4 3 2 1

Mfr: TIMS / Shenzhen, China / February 2016 / PO# 9372642

Table of Contents

Foreword

After writing about the importance of helping our children hear from God by memorizing Scripture in her successful book *I Can Learn the Bible*, Holly now leads us to teach our children how to talk to God. Prayer, like any form of communication, is a two-way street. God speaks to us through the Bible, and we speak to Him through prayer. Like ham and eggs, peanut butter and jelly, and pancakes and syrup, receiving God's Word in our hearts and offering our prayers to Him go together.

God must surely delight in the simple yet heart-driven prayers emitting from little minds and hearts that are pure in motive as well as morals. I can still hear, ringing in my mind, Holly's own sweet petitions to God as she was learning to frame syllables into words and sentences. Now, as an adult, she has beaten out these prayer principles on the anvil of personal experience, teaching her four children to pray with power and expectancy to a God who said, "A little child will lead them" (Isaiah 11:6).

Disclaimer: I am a bit partial. As Holly's dad I have watched her consistently show maturity beyond her years. She writes from a platform of credibility and integrity. The wisdom of this book, borne out of her experience at the foot of her good and godly mom, has been passed on to her own children and to those who read and heed these words. In case you haven't guessed by now, I am really proud to be Holly's dad!

—O.S. Hawkins, author of *The Joshua Code*, *The Jesus Code*, *The James Code*, and *VIP: Learning to Influence with Vision, Integrity, and Purpose*

A Note to Parents

Is there a better sound in all the world than the sound of a child's prayer? Why is that? I believe it is because children have the ability to connect with God simply and effectively. There is something about a child talking to God that makes Him seem so real and tangible.

We would be hard-pressed to find a subject in the Bible of greater importance than prayer. If God's Word is how He talks to us, prayer is how we talk to God. How can we possibly expect to have any level of relationship with God without communication with Him? Prayer is a crucial, central part of the Christian life, and it is just as applicable for children as it is for adults.

Once, after Jesus finished praying alone, one of His disciples said, "Lord, please teach us how to pray" (Luke 11:1). The wording of his request is significant. He didn't say, "Remind us to pray," or "Encourage us to pray." No, he asked Jesus to *teach* them how to pray. Prayer is learned. Even many of us who have known God for years sometimes wander aimlessly in our prayer lives. And we often expect our children to know automatically how to navigate talking to God. The Bible is very clear about why and how we ought to pray. What better time to learn how to pray than during childhood, when habits that will last a lifetime are formed?

This fifty-two-week, parent-led study will teach children how to pray, how to listen, and what it means to draw near to God. We will tackle subjects like the importance of a thankful heart, how to "praise," why we must confess, and where to go for help. We will talk about how to "be still," we will look at the prayers Jesus prayed, and in the end, we will all be changed! Not only will this book give children the tools they need to understand prayer, it will also help them grow in their understanding of God and build intimacy with Him along the way. Your child will need a blank journal, and will often need a parent to guide them through these activities.

Remember that your children are watching you. Seeing a praying parent can be a powerful experience for a child. Watching you pray will have far greater impact than any book they read or sermon they hear. They will learn from you, and you will learn from them. In Matthew 19:14, Jesus said, "Let the little children come to Me, and do not forbid them; for of such is the kingdom of heaven" (NKJV). And oh how I love the next phrase in verse 15, which so beautifully describes Jesus' connection to children: "And He laid His hands on them."

I pray even now in my heart for your family and

this journey you begin today . . . a journey that will lead you closer to the heart of God. May He lay His hands on you and your children as His Word becomes alive and His voice whispers to you. Let us pray!

Jesus, I just want to talk to You. You are a great big God, but I know You are my Friend and You are listening.

Week 1

All About Prayer

Try to guess what all of these things have in common: a text message, sign language, a phone call, and a walkie-talkie.

These are all things people use to communicate with each other. But how do people communicate with God? By using a "tool" He gave us—prayer! Let's answer some important questions about prayer.

Who?

Prayer is between you and God. When you pray, you are actually talking to the God of the universe. Stop and think about that . . . *you are talking to this great big God who made the world and made you, the God who placed the stars in the sky and brings the sun up every morning.* That is quite a thought! Even though God does all of those things, He is also your friend (Revelation 3:20).

What?

What is *prayer*? If you said, "Talking to God and hearing Him talk to you," you were right! It really is that simple. Prayer is telling God how you are feeling and what is on your mind. Sometimes prayer means just being still and quiet. It is thinking about God and listening to His voice in your heart (Jeremiah 33:3).

Where and When?

Where and when can you pray? You can pray anywhere and anytime! That is the wonderful thing about God: He is *always* there for you. You might pray in your bed, in the shower, in the car, or at the dinner table. You can pray in the morning, in the middle of the night, or anytime in between. There is never a time or place where God cannot hear your prayers (Psalm 139:7–10).

Why?

Who is your closest friend? What would happen if you could never talk to that person again? Just like you cannot have a relationship with a friend without talking and listening, you cannot have a relationship with God without talking and listening to Him. The most important reason we pray is so that we can know God (James 4:8).

Praying This Week:

Practice just talking to God. Don't worry about what you think you "should" say; just say whatever comes to your mind. Jesus cares much more about what is in your heart (the things you are really feeling and thinking) than what you think you are "supposed" to say. Tell Him about something in your life that makes you happy or sad. When you are finished talking, be very quiet, listen with your heart, and see if you think God is saying anything to you. Last, have your mom or dad get you a blank journal. You will use the journal to write down different prayers as you read this book.

Father, help me to pray every day . . . and to remember that You love me no matter what!

The Best Habit

Biting your nails, blowing bubbles with chewing gum, chewing on pencils, not making your bed . . . do any of those habits sound familiar? What are some of your good and bad habits? A habit is something you do so many times, it's almost like you can't stop! If you develop a good habit, like praying, great things can happen.

Everyday Prayers

The apostle Paul told new believers in Jesus, "Never stop praying" (1 Thessalonians 5:17). He knew that he could pray all the time. In fact, Paul's whole day could be one long prayer. He could wake up talking to God and fall asleep still talking to God. (Of course, he would take some breaks in between!)

Here are ways you could make prayer a habit:

- Find a "prayer friend." This is someone who will pray with you and for you, and who will remind you to pray when you might forget or get too busy.

19

- Write your prayers in your journal. This will help you to focus on what you want to say to God, so your mind doesn't wander! You can also keep a prayer list in your journal.
- Pray in your bed. Every night before you fall asleep, let your last words and thoughts be directed toward Jesus.
- Set an alarm to remind you. You could have it ring a few minutes earlier than usual in the morning, so you can pray before your day begins.

No-Matter-What Love

True or false: "The more I pray, the more God will love me." False! You see, we always need to be reminded that God loves us no matter what we do. If you prayed only

one time a year or twenty times a day, God would love you exactly the same. (And believe me, it's *a lot* of love!) We don't pray so that God will love us more; we pray so that we can know Him. We pray so that He can help us when we need it, and so that our minds can be focused on Him, not on all the bad stuff that happens in this world.

Praying This Week:

Ask God to help you make prayer a habit. Pray that He will remind you when you might forget and that He will help you *want* to pray every day. Tell Him you want to know Him more and that you need Him to lead you and guide you. Also practice praying at the same time each day. You will soon have a new habit . . . the best habit of all!

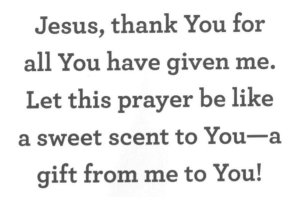

Jesus, thank You for
all You have given me.
Let this prayer be like
a sweet scent to You—a
gift from me to You!

A Gift to God

Have a parent help you light a candle that smells nice, or spritz a scented room spray or perfume. Talk about how it makes you feel when you first smell the special scent.

The Greatest Giver

Can you remember any reasons why it is good to pray? We pray so that we can know God and hear Him speak. We also pray so that we can share our hearts with Him and have our minds focused on Him.

See if you can guess another good reason to pray based on what James 1:17 says: "Every perfect gift is from God. These good gifts come down from the Creator of the sun, moon, and stars." Think about it. God has given you a family, a home, food, clothing, and things to enjoy. He has blessed you with life, and most of all, He has given His only Son so that you can spend forever with Him. So prayer is one thing that we, as God's children, can give back to God! It is like an offering, or gift, just for Him.

Something Sweet for God

In the days of the Bible, people would burn something called *incense*. Incense produces a very good smell after it is burned. In Psalm 141:2, David prayed, "Let my prayer be like incense placed before you." In other words, "Let my prayer be something sweet to You—something You enjoy and that makes You happy." In Revelation 5:8, the Bible even describes the prayers of God's people as golden bowls full of incense before His throne. Just like the smell you are surrounded with right now can make you feel good, your prayers to God can be a delight to Him.

Can we be sure that God hears us when we pray? Read these verses out loud: 1 John 5:14; Psalm 3:4; 34:15; 55:16–17; 86:7; 91:15.

God hears when you pray!

Praying This Week:

Continue making a habit of talking to God every day. Remember that your prayers reach Him and that they are like a sweet smell to Him. Thank God for all He has given you, and tell Him you want your prayers to be your gift to Him.

Father, I know You have told
me in Your Word to pray. I want
to obey You and come to You every
day, asking for this one thing . . .

God's Command

Use a coin to play heads or tails with someone in your family. Keep playing until one person wins three times in a row. It might take awhile, but keep trying!

A Judge and a Widow

In Luke 18, Jesus told a story to help His followers understand why it is important not to give up praying. In this story there was a judge who did not love God or people, and there was a widow (a woman whose husband has died) who kept coming to this judge. She told the judge that someone was not being fair to her, and she wanted the judge to make this person be fair. But the judge did not want to help her. The widow kept asking and pleading, and did not give up. Finally, the judge was so bothered by the widow that, even though he didn't actually care about her situation, he gave her what she wanted because she was wearing him out!

Jesus told His disciples that God wants His people to come to Him over and over, like that widow did. If a

27

bad judge gave the woman what she needed, won't a good God give us what we need? (And just a reminder: we do not always get what we ask for, since it may not be God's best plan for us.)

God's Best

So here is yet another reason to pray . . . God says to! And if God says this is something we should do, that is reason enough to do it. Look up the following verses, and see how God commands us to pray: Romans 12:12; Ephesians 6:18; Philippians 4:6; Colossians 4:2; 1 Thessalonians 5:17.

All throughout the Bible, we see examples of God's people praying and commands from God for us to pray. God tells us to pray not so that He can give us a rule to follow, but because He knows that is what is best for us. We are blessed through prayer as we hear Him speak to us and come to know Him better.

Praying This Week:

Try praying for the same thing every day. You could ask God to help you be kind to your brother or sister, or to help you not be scared or anxious about something. Write this one request in your journal, and read it before you pray—it will help you remember to keep asking, just like the widow.

Jesus, help me to learn more about You. Show me who You are, and pull me close to You.

Knowing God

What is your favorite thing you own? Maybe it is a doll, a basketball, or a blanket. Without looking at the item, describe it in detail to your family. Talk about its characteristics: Is it big or small? Soft or hard? What color is it? Does it have a smell? Why is this item special and different from other things you own? Now, get the item and show your family what you were describing.

When you have something you love, you spend a lot of time with it, and you begin to discover things about it that you didn't notice before. In the same way, when we spend time talking to God, we begin to learn new things about Him and find out more about what He is like. *That is knowing God.*

How to Know God

What is the difference between knowing *about* someone and *knowing* someone? You might know a lot about your favorite singers or athletes—their accomplishments, maybe things they like to do. But do you *know* them? Could you say what makes them laugh or cry, or what they care most about? Do you know them like you know your mom or dad? Probably not. You cannot really know someone without spending time listening to and talking with them. This is why it is so important for us to pray . . . so we can know God.

If you wonder whether you really can get to know God, listen to something Jesus said right before He went to the cross and finished the work God had for Him to do. He prayed, "This is eternal life: that men can know you, the only true God, and that men can know Jesus Christ, the One you sent" (John 17:3). Jesus is telling us clearly that we can actually know Him!

Who He Is

What kinds of things might you learn about God as you know Him more? You might learn that He is patient and kind, or that He is in control. You might

learn that He loves you with a love that is greater than you can imagine! The more you know God, the more you will want to know Him. And that is what spending "forever" with Him is all about.

Praying This Week:

Tell God you want to know Him more. Ask Him to show you something specific about who He is. Concentrate on one thing, like His love, His faithfulness, or His forgiveness, while you pray. Remember that the more you pray, the more you will know Him.

Lord, I need You. You are God and I am not. I don't want to try to live my life without You!

Week 6

needing God

Put on a blindfold and have someone in your family walk you around the house. When you are finished, talk about these things: How much did you need to feel the person's hand leading you? Did you want to let go? Did you know where you were going? Could you have gotten there and back on your own?

Wearing that blindfold is a little bit like living in this world. Sometimes we think we can handle it on our own, but the truth is, we need God to guide us. He can see things that we can't see, and He knows things that we don't know. So we have to depend on Him to lead us.

Being Humble

Here is one more reason to pray: Prayer keeps us *humble*. Do you know what that word means? If you are humble, then you understand that you can't do everything on your own. You realize that you are not the greatest, smartest, most talented person on earth, and that you are pretty small compared to God! And you know that anything good you do is because God helped you.

Read these verses about staying humble out loud: Ephesians 4:2; Philippians 2:3; James 4:10; 1 Peter 5:6.

Remembering God

Sometimes, we might get too busy and forget to pray. Other times, we might not feel like praying so we choose to do something else instead. In those times, we start to think that we don't need God. But that's not true at all! We especially need God when we're busy or don't feel like talking to Him. When we pray, we are showing that there is someone bigger and higher than us. We are reminding ourselves that we are not in control and that we need God! When we tell

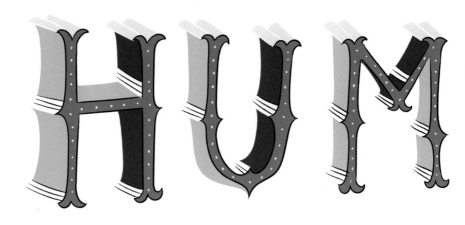

Him that we can't make it in this crazy world without Him, we remember that we depend on Him.

Praying This Week:

Try praying on your knees. This will help you remember that God is much bigger and stronger than you and that you need His help. It will keep you humble before Him. It will also tell God that you know He is the only true God and that you trust Him.

Jesus, I pray in Your name.
I know it is because
of You that God can
hear my prayers.

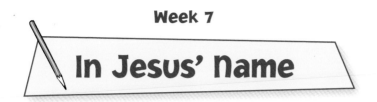

Week 7

In Jesus' Name

Grab a piece of paper, a pencil, and some markers or crayons. As a family, make a drawing of a large castle. It can be decorated however you choose, but make sure that there is only one door to the castle. No one can get in through any windows or back doors—*only one entrance.*

Think of that castle as being God. There is only one way for us, people who mess up and who are always sinning, to be able to talk to God through prayer. Do you know what (or who) that one way is? Do you know who the door to the castle represents?

Jesus Is the Way

In John 14:6, Jesus said, "I am the way. And I am the truth and the life. The only way to the Father is through me." Because of our sin, we must be separated from God. But do you remember what God did about that? He sent His Son, Jesus, to be punished for our sin on the cross. So Jesus was separated from God instead of us. Jesus didn't stay separated from

God though—three days after He died, He rose again. Because of all of that, we can now get to God! But we can't do it on our own—we can only reach Him by believing and trusting in Jesus. Jesus is the only way to God. Jesus is the door to the castle. So when we pray "in Jesus' name," we are telling God that because of Jesus, we know He hears our prayers.

Our High Priest

In Hebrews 4:14, the apostle Paul said that Jesus is a "great high priest." A priest is someone who is holy and follows God's laws. He also helps people to tell God about things they have done wrong and to pray to God. Paul said that Jesus is our true "High Priest" because He takes our prayers and presents them to the Father. Praying "in Jesus' name" reminds us that He does this for us!

Praying This Week:

Write John 14:6 in your prayer journal and keep it near a place where you like to pray. Try to keep reading and practicing this verse until you can say it by heart. Tell God that you are praying in the name of Jesus. And remember: you know *the way*!

Father, I come
to You in a
secret place today.
I'm so glad You
are here with me.

Praying in Secret

Have each person in your family say a prayer out loud. Then have everyone pray silently for a few minutes. When you are finished, talk about the difference between praying out loud and praying in silence. Which way do you prefer and why? What felt different about each way?

Big, Fancy Words

Jesus talked to His followers about people who only pray when others can hear them, because they want other people to think they are great at praying. They use big words and talk loudly so everyone will notice them. Jesus said not to be like those people. He said that when you pray, you should go into your room and shut your door. He said that you should not use big, crazy words, but rather just talk your usual way! If you do that, God will hear you in that secret place, and He will reward you.

Jesus had a name for those people who like to pray for everyone to hear: hypocrites. Have you ever heard that word before? A *hypocrite* is someone who says one thing but acts another way. They want people to think they are a certain way, but really they are not that way at all. Hypocrites care more about what people think than what God thinks. When we pray in a secret place and no one can hear us but God, it pleases Him. We show that we care most about what He thinks.

Praying with Each Other

Now, it's important to know that God is not saying it is bad if other people hear you pray. He is saying that your *reason* for praying should be not for other people to hear you, but for God to hear you. This also doesn't mean God does not like for us to pray with

others. Jesus actually said in Matthew 18:20, "If two or three people come together in my name, I am there with them." He likes for us to agree with each other and pray for the same thing together. There is power in that!

Praying This Week:

Where do you like to pray? Do you have a favorite chair or place you like to sit? Do you have a favorite hiding place in your house? Pick a spot and pray in the same place every day. Make sure it is a private place where only God can hear you. Also, if you pray with a family member or friend, remember Jesus' promise that He is right there with you.

Lord, I come to You today, and before anything else, I say thank You.

Week 9

Enter with Thanksgiving

Pretend you are a king or queen. Try to make a throne in the biggest chair you can find, and see if you can find some kind of crown. Have each person in your family enter the room one at a time, and have them greet you like they would greet royalty. They might bow, say something kind, or bring you a gift.

Honor and Respect

Just as we would greet a king or queen with kindness, Psalm 100 reminds us to enter into God's presence with a thankful heart. In fact, verse 4 says, "Come into his city with songs of thanksgiving." Even though we know we can talk to God anytime and anywhere, we need to remember that it is a big privilege to do this. God is not one of your school buddies or someone to whom you might yell, "Hey, dude! What's up?" He is *God*, and showing Him respect shows Him that we love Him and want to treat Him differently than we treat just anyone.

Imagine you were invited to the White House to meet the president. Would you burst through the doors, give a high five, and right away start asking the president for things you want to be changed? Of course not! You would walk in politely, show respect, and maybe say something kind. If we would treat the president, who is just a person, that way, shouldn't we show even more respect to God, who is the Maker and Ruler of all? So when we enter into God's presence, when we come to Him in prayer, the first thing we should do is say "thank You."

A List of Thanks

In the weeks ahead, we are going to talk about many things we can be thankful for. Start brainstorming now about all the things you have been given. Remember, God is the giver of every gift in your life. First, practice by telling each person in your family "thank you" for something they have done or given to you. Then make a list with your family of everything you would like to thank God for. Start with something like your home. It will be a long list, I'm sure!

Praying This Week:

When you wake up in the morning, let the first words out of your mouth be, "Thank You, God!" Write Psalm 100 in your prayer journal, and read it every day this week. Begin each of your prayers by thanking God for something He has given to you or done for you.

Jesus, You have given
me a family and people
who love me. Thank You
for each one of them!

Thanks for My People

Identify the smallest person in your family (maybe it's you!), and then wrap them up like a present. You could use toilet paper, wrapping paper, a big box, or whatever you can find. Then put a bow or ribbon on top of their head. Do they look funny? As you look at that silly present, remember that each person in your family is God's gift to you.

We Need Each Other

In Genesis 2, we see that after God created everything, He formed the first man, Adam, out of dust. God said something interesting about Adam in verse 18: "It is not good for the man to be alone. I will make a helper who is right for him." It was then that the first family came to be: Adam and Eve. God knew that people need people. He knew that Adam would be better off if he had someone else with him in the garden. Adam could enjoy all of creation and every animal under the sun, but that was not enough.

In the same way, God knows that you need people,

and He has blessed you and given them to you, just as He did Adam. We are not meant to live our lives without others.

Who are your "people"? In your prayer journal, write down about five or six names of the people you know best. This will probably be your family members and maybe a couple of close friends. Think of those people as gifts God has given you. Have you thanked God for those gifts in your life? Can you imagine what your life would be like without them?

God Sees

Sometimes the people God puts in our lives can do things to hurt our hearts. This happens because people are not perfect, and they mess up a lot. That is why we all need Jesus. It's important to remember that even when bad things happen and our people do something that we don't like, God knows. Nothing that happens to you is out of His hands. He can even take those bad things and fit them into His perfect plan for you.

Praying This Week:

Thank God for a different person each day. Pick one or two of the names you wrote down on the list of your people, and write them a note, telling them that you are thanking God for them. Tell them why you are so glad God gave them to you.

Jesus, thank You for the
ways that You keep me healthy.
I'm sorry when I forget!

Thanks for My Health

Play a matching game. If you don't have one, have a parent help you make one with small pieces of paper. Who was the best at remembering where the matches were? Was it easy to forget?

It's very easy to forget about ways God has blessed us. We take for granted things that we can do all the time. "Taking something for granted" means forgetting about what you have. It means not being thankful, or not thinking about ways God has blessed you because you are so used to them.

I'm Thankful for . . .

We often take our health for granted. What are some things about your health you can thank God for? Can you see? Can you hear? Can you walk or run? Are you breathing? Do you have food to eat that keeps you healthy? Water to drink? Talk about some other things related to your health you can be thankful for.

Did you know that Jesus thanked God for His food? John 6:11 says, "Jesus took the loaves of bread. He thanked God for the bread and gave it to the people who were sitting there. He did the same with the fish. He gave them as much as they wanted." Also, when He was having His last meal with His disciples, "Jesus took some bread. He thanked God for it and broke it" (Matthew 26:26).

What About Sickness?

Does God promise us that we will always be healthy? Not at all. In fact, this world is full of sickness and disease and unhealthy people. I'm sure you know people in your life (maybe even you) who are sick in different ways. It is a good reminder that this earth is not really

our home. It's not the best place to be. In heaven, we will have new bodies. No sickness is ever allowed there!

If there is something about your health that you wish were different, you can tell God that too. Ask Him to help you in the ways you are not healthy as you keep thanking Him for the ways you are.

Praying This Week:

Every day, think of one way you are healthy. Say a prayer thanking God for it, and try to think about it all day. For instance, you might say, "Thank You, Lord, that I can use my legs." And every time you run or jump that day, you can have that in your mind and thank God in your heart.

God, You made me special. I thank You for the things I can do!

Thanks for My Talents

Sit in a circle with your family, and put one person in the middle. Then have everyone in the circle talk about things the person in the middle can do well. These could be things like art, sports, music, and reading. Or they could be things like caring about others, being a servant, being a leader, being organized, and being generous.

Your Gifts

The things that you do well are also gifts from God to you. God wants you to use those gifts to bless other people and to point other people to Him. Listen to what Jesus said to His followers about this:

> You are the light that gives light to the world. A city that is built on a hill cannot be hidden. And people don't hide a light under a bowl. They put the light on a lampstand. Then the light shines for all the people in the house. In the same way, you should be a light for other people. Live so that they will see

the good things you do. Live so that they will praise your Father in heaven. (Matthew 5:14-16)

So if you are good at something, Jesus wants you to use it to show others His love. Do good things, using either your talents or character traits, so you can bless others and show them how great God is. And be sure to thank God for the gifts and talents He has given you!

David's Gift

When David was young and took care of sheep, he liked to play the harp. He was very musical, and he used that gift to honor God. He would sing songs of praise to God. He would also use his gift to bless others. King Saul had become very sad and upset. He would ask for David, and David would come play his

harp for King Saul. After he played, Saul would feel better. David was using the gifts God had given him well (1 Samuel 16:23).

In your prayer journal, write down a few of the gifts or talents you think God has given you. Think about some ways that you can use those gifts to show God to others. Talk about that with your family. Then pray together, thanking God for all of His gifts.

Praying This Week:

Start by thanking God for the ways He has made you special. Ask Him to show you how to use the gifts He's given you. When you find yourself using your talents or gifts, remember to thank God that He has given them to you.

THANK YOU

Lord, You
have given me
the greatest gift
I will ever receive,
and so I say thank You.

Thanks for Jesus

Lie on the floor with your family members and try to spell out the letters *J-E-S-U-S* by using only your bodies. You might have to do one letter at a time. Have someone take a picture from above you so you can see what you look like!

Now answer some of these questions: What do you know about Jesus? What was Jesus like? Did He live like a king? What were some of the things He taught about? What made Him different from other people? What did He care about most? Who were His friends? What was His purpose for being on earth? Do you know Him?

No Greater Gift

Paul said in 2 Corinthians 9:15, "Thanks be to God for his gift that is too wonderful to explain." What would you guess he was talking about? It is the same gift given to you: Jesus. You will be given many gifts in your life—gifts from God, from your family, and from your friends. But there is no greater gift you will ever receive than the gift of Jesus.

Why?

Do you remember what John 3:16 says? "For God loved the world *so much* that he gave his only Son. God gave his Son so that whoever believes in him may not be lost, but have eternal life." The reason this gift is so special is that without Jesus coming to die on the cross and take the punishment for our sins, we could not spend forever with God in heaven. Not only that, but we have the gift of Jesus with us every day, as He talks to us and walks with us and teaches us to love Him. So . . . if this is the greatest gift you have ever been given, wouldn't it be a good idea to thank God for it? I think so too!

Praying This Week:

Write this poem in your journal. Read it each day and make it your prayer:

I've been given many things,
some small, some big, some bright;
A hand to hold and food to eat,
a bed for sleep at night.
Of all the gifts that I can name
there is one standing tall;
It's Jesus and His love for me—
the greatest Gift of all!
So thank You for this Gift, oh Lord;
I'm grateful to You now.
I know one day I'll see Your face
and on my knees I'll bow.
You'll run to me and hold me close
and never let me go;
I'll hold on tight and stay with You—
the greatest Gift I know.

Jesus, thank You for
the light of Your Word
that shows me the way.

HOPE

STRENGTH

COMFORT

WISDOM

Thanks for Your Word

Find a flashlight and go into the darkest room of the house. Have a parent put something small, like a coin, on the floor on the opposite side of the room. First, try to find the item without the flashlight. Then use the flashlight to find it. Did having the light down by your feet make all the difference? What if you had to walk around in the dark every day without a light? Would you ever know where you were going? How would you know the way?

A Dark Place

Psalm 119:105 says, "Your word is like a lamp for my feet and a light for my way." What do you think that means? As hard as it is to think about, living in this world can be like walking around in a dark room. Since there is sin in this world, it is very easy for us to lose our way. We might think we know where to go or what to do, but really we are just wandering around in a dark world. Trying to hear from God and obey Him can sometimes seem as hard as finding a coin in a dark room. We need a light to show the way!

God fixed that problem by giving us His Word—the Bible. Since we have this Book that tells us how to live, where to go, and what to do with our lives, we don't have to be lost! His Word lights the way. Like that flashlight, the Bible shows our feet where to go and leads us to our treasure . . . God.

The Light That Guides Us

Psalm 119 is all about God's Word. It's a pretty long chapter, but it's a wonderful one to read. It tells us why we should be thankful for God's Word. Here are some of the reasons: It keeps us from sinning (v. 11), it gives us advice (v. 24), and it makes us strong (v. 28). It gives us freedom (v. 45) and hope (v. 49), it comforts us (v. 52), and it makes us wise (v. 66). It lasts forever (v. 89), it is sweet like honey (v. 103), it is right and fair (v. 137), and it is trustworthy (v. 147).

Praying This Week:

Spend time each day reading a few verses out of Psalm 119. Then thank God for His Word and for not letting you wander around in the dark. Be thankful for the Light that guides your way.

Father, thank You for the hard things in my life. I trust You with them, and I know You will help me through.

Thanks for My Troubles

Play a "rescue" game. Have each person in your family pretend that they are sinking in quicksand. Have a parent be the "rescuer" and pull each person out of the sand one by one. Then talk about this: Did you feel safe once the rescuer was holding on to you? Did you feel close to them and thankful for them?

Sometimes we go through hard times in life, and God comes alongside us. He pulls us up into His arms and holds us close. Maybe you or someone you know is sick. Maybe there are problems in your family. Maybe you didn't make a team, or you are feeling alone or left out. There are many things that can give us trouble in life.

A Good Father

Have you ever heard of saying "thank you" for something that hurts you? Does that seem crazy? The truth is, we *can* thank God even for the hard times, because good things come from them. When we struggle, we can really tell that He is with us, and we get to know

71

Him and love Him more. Our troubles make us run to God, and He shows us in those times what a good, wonderful, loving Father He is.

Jesus by Your Side

If there is something you are going through today that is hard and makes you sad, God has something to tell you. Imagine Jesus pulling you up into His lap and saying this:

Don't be afraid, because I have saved you. I have called you by name, and *you are mine*. When you pass through the waters, I will be with you. When you cross rivers, you will not drown. When you walk through fire, you will not be burned. The flames will not hurt you. This is because I, the Lord, am your God. I, the Holy One of Israel, am your Savior. (Isaiah 43:1–3)

When troubles come, Jesus is walking beside you and will never let go of your hand. Trust Him today and thank Him for the good things that will come from your troubles.

Praying This Week:

Pick one thing in your life that makes you sad or mad, and pray about it every day this week. Tell God that you trust Him and that you want to run to Him for help. Thank Him for never letting you go.

Jesus, You are God, and You are great. If we don't praise You, creation will!

Week 16

What Is Praise?

Who is someone you admire? Say three different things about why you admire that person and what makes them special, and then have every family member take a turn doing the same.

Admiring God

Just like you were saying those things about the person you admire, the Bible tells us to do that for God. To *praise* means to say good things about someone. It means to give thanks to God or express love for Him. When you are praising God, you are telling Him that He is great and wonderful and better than anything. You are telling Him how much you love Him, and you are worshipping Him. Psalm 92:1 says, "It is good to praise the Lord, to sing praises to God Most High." Praising God reminds us of who He is and all He has done for us. Did you know that even creation itself offers praise to God?

Creation's Praise

Read Psalm 148 and talk about all the different parts of creation that offer Him praise. Can you imagine the sun praising God? The waters, the mountains, the rocks? One time when Jesus was coming into Jerusalem, people who had seen His great works were shouting praises to Him. Some Pharisees told Jesus to make them stop, but Jesus said, "I tell you, if my followers don't say these things, then the stones will cry out" (Luke 19:40). Wow! God is so worthy of our praise that if we do not give it to Him, creation will.

God is bigger and better than our minds could ever understand. Giving Him praise reminds us that He is good, powerful, wise, faithful, full of mercy and love . . . and much, much more.

Praying This Week:

Do you have a favorite praise song? It can be any song that talks about God and how great He is. Begin your time of prayer each day by singing a song of praise to God. You could do this with your family or by yourself. As you are singing, try to picture Jesus smiling down at you, enjoying your praise.

Lord, You are such a good Father!
Help me remember Your goodness
no matter what comes my way.

You Are Good

Do you like chocolate? If you had a chocolate bar and someone broke it up into small pieces, would you still eat it? Would it still taste the same? What if someone melted the chocolate? Would it still taste good then? Yes, I think it would! God is a good God, no matter what happens in our lives. One of the ways we can give praise to God in prayer is by telling Him how *good* He is. Can you think of some reasons why God is good? Talk about those with your family.

When Things Are Bad

Sometimes in life, you may not feel like God is good. You may think things like, *Why did God let this happen? Why didn't God answer my prayer?* It's okay to wonder about those things. Most people do. But we must be careful not to let our hearts become angry with God. We need to trust that God is good, no matter what happens in our lives. Just as the chocolate tastes good no matter how you serve it, God is good no matter what bad things may come.

Job's Story

There was a man named Job who followed God and stayed away from anything evil. He was good at doing the right thing, and God loved him. Satan told God that Job only did those things because God had blessed him with so much. He told God that if everything was taken away, Job would stop loving, honoring, and following God. So God gave Satan permission to take things away from Job. Job lost his animals, servants, and even his own family. He suffered greatly and lost his health and all he had. In all of this, he remembered that even though bad things were happening to him, God was still good.

There are many things that will change in your life. You will get older and all sorts of things will happen—some good and some bad. Your life will take new twists and turns. But there is one thing that will never change, and that is *who God is*. "Jesus Christ is the same yesterday, today, and forever" (Hebrews 13:8).

Praying This Week:

Focus on the goodness of God. Each day that you pray, think of one way God has been good to you. If there are things in your life that are confusing, and you don't *feel* as though God is good in those situations, tell Him that too. Ask Him to help you remember that He is good all the time, no matter what.

FRIENDS

FAMILY

PETS

HEALTH

SCHOOL

Jesus, I don't deserve the good things You do for me, and I praise You today for Your grace.

You Show Grace

Can you make a paper chain? Have each person in your family make their own chain with a few circles. Place your hands in two of those circles as if they were handcuffs. Try to do a couple normal activities, like combing your hair. Then, on a count of three, have everyone break out of their chains at the same time. Talk about how it feels to be free.

Grace from God

Do you know what *grace* is? *Grace* means getting something that you do not deserve. It's a little bit like coming in last place in a race, but getting the first-place trophy. Can you think of ways that God gives us grace? God did not have to do anything for us or give anything to us, but He chose to save us and to give His Son for us. He chose to leave His Holy Spirit here on earth with us. Ephesians 2:5-7 says:

> We were spiritually dead because of the things we did wrong against God. But God gave us new life

with Christ. You have been saved by God's grace. And he raised us up with Christ and gave us a seat with him in the heavens. He did this for those of us who are in Christ Jesus. He did this so that for all future time he could show the very great riches of his grace. He shows that grace by being kind to us in Christ Jesus.

Starting Over

Perhaps the most beautiful thing about God is the grace He offers us. And God not only offered us grace when Jesus died for us—He gives it to us each and every day. Have you ever had a day when you wanted to just ask for a "do-over"? Maybe you said something you wish you hadn't, or you made a wrong choice. Maybe your attitude was awful, or you just couldn't be patient, as hard as you tried. Days like that can be hard, but all days come to an end. After you fall asleep, something wonderful happens: you get a new day. The sun rises, you open your eyes, and it's like God is saying,

"Okay, do-over!" He forgives us of our sin and gives us a brand-new start every day. That is grace . . . and that is a reason to praise Him!

Praying This Week:

Keep thinking about the word *grace*. See if you can find a way to show grace to someone in your life by doing something kind for them. You might give up your turn in a game to someone who has already had a turn or share your favorite dessert with your brother who already ate his! Then write about it in your journal. As you are praying, remember to praise God for the grace He gives you, fully and freely.

Your love, oh Lord, is higher
than the heavens. It's so deep
and wide . . . it never stops!

You Are Love

How many names do you answer to? What about your parents or siblings? Grandparents? Spend some time talking about the names in your family. We are usually known by more than one name, and the same is true for God.

Do you know how the Bible describes God in 1 John 4:8? It says, "God is love." Think about that. It doesn't simply say God *loves* . . . it says God *is* love! That means that loving is not just something God does, but it is who He is. God is always loving; it is His nature.

A Love That Never Stops

Sometimes we describe God's love as "unfailing." This means that the love of God is something that will never run out, will never give up, and will never disappear. In Jeremiah 31:3, God said, "I love you people with a love that will last forever. I became your friend because of my love and kindness." You will have people in your life who love you. They will tell you they love you and show you they love you. And they do! But the thing is, they are just people, and they are not able to love with this "forever" kind of love like God is. He is the only One who loves you with a perfect, holy, unfailing, and forever love.

Praising God for His love tells Him that we see and feel His love. We know it is there, and we think it is wonderful that He can have *this much love* for us. We want to tell Him how amazing it is that He showed us His love by sending His Son to die for us.

A Love That Never Changes

Now, there is one more thing we often forget. Does God love you because of the good things you do? No! Does He love you more when you pray a lot and spend time with Him? Certainly not! God's love is always there *no matter what.*

Praying is important because it reminds us that God is there, and it allows us to praise Him for who He is. This brings God delight, but it does not make Him love us more. There is nothing you can do that would make God love you any more than He already does. And there is nothing you could do to make God love you less. Let's praise God for His amazing love today!

Praying This Week:

Write Ephesians 3:18-19 in your prayer journal, and read it each day before you pray. When you are praying, tell God how great His love is. Tell Him that no one could ever love you the way He loves you. Praise Him because His love never gives up.

Father, You can do anything!
You are such a big, strong,
great, loving God.

GREAT

You Are Great

We use the word *great* for all kinds of things. You might have had a great pizza for dinner. Or maybe you did a great job on a test or in a game. But when we use the word *great* to describe God, it means much, much more.

Our Great God

God is the Creator and Ruler over the entire universe. He made everything out of nothing. His voice thunders through the heavens, and His majesty and power never come to an end. He placed the stars in the sky and named each of them. He told the oceans where to start and where to stop. He holds the world together. God has always been, and He always will be. He is not just "here" or "there" at different times, but everywhere all the time! He knows everything there is to know, and He has more power than anyone or anything. God is bigger, stronger, lovelier, and more mind-blowing than we can even understand.

Not only that, but He made you! He loves you with a forever love. He knows everything there is to know about you. He hears your prayers and He rejoices over them. (This is a bit different from great pizza, right?)

Can You Hear It?

In Revelation 19, John described what it will be like when we are forever with God. He said that there will be so many voices singing "Hallelujah!" that it will sound like roaring waters. All of the angels and those of us who know God will be gathered around His throne, singing praises to Him. What a sound that will be! Can you close your eyes and imagine what that might be like? God is truly great, and He deserves our praise.

Praying This Week:

Reading through the Psalms is a great way to praise God. Pick one of the psalms each day and read about how wonderful and majestic He is. As you pray, tell God about some of the things you think are amazing about Him. Tell Him what a great God He is and how happy you are to know Him.

Lord, I praise You
because You watch
over me. I know I don't
have to be afraid.

You Protect Me

Build a fort with your family. Make sure it is big enough so that everyone can get inside. Use furniture, couch pillows, blankets, and anything else you can find. When you are inside the fort, talk about some ways that God has protected you and your family.

God Our Fortress

The word *fort* comes from the word *fortress*, which is a place that is protected and helps you defend against attack. If you were expecting an army to invade your territory, you would build a fortress, a place where you could go and no one could get in. It would protect you against your enemies. The Bible often describes God as our fortress. We can run to Him and He will protect us.

When David was running from Saul and other people who wanted to kill him, he would often sing songs of praise to God. In 2 Samuel 22:3, he sang, "My God is my rock. I can run to him for safety. He is my shield and my saving strength. The Lord is my high tower and my place of safety." David knew that no one could watch over him like God. In Psalm 23, David said that the Lord was like a shepherd to him. God gave him everything he needed, and he never had to be afraid because the Lord was *always* with him. Have you ever praised God for protecting you and watching over you?

Angels All Around

God is protecting you even when you don't know it. His Word says that He has put His angels in charge of you, to protect you (Psalm 91:11)! Can you imagine that—angels all around you, watching over you? But wait: Just because God promises to protect us, does that mean nothing bad or scary will ever happen to us? No, it doesn't. God promises to watch over us, but sometimes He allows troubles to come into our lives. It's not really our job to understand why God allows certain things to happen. Do you know what our job is? It's to trust Him! Your job is to trust that He is watching over you and that He will always do what is right for you.

Praying This Week:

Have you ever been in a situation where you were very afraid? What kinds of things make you scared? Write about those things in your prayer journal. Praise God in your prayers for how He has protected you. Talk about specific things, and tell Him that He is your strong tower, your fortress, and your protector.

Father, I praise You today for making me.

You made me just the way You wanted me to be.

You Made Me

See if you can find two of the same kind of coin. They could be two pennies or two dimes, as long as they are worth the same. Now, look closely at them. What is different about them? Is one of them darker? One of them older? Is one of them smoother than the other? Just as those coins are the same but different, God made people the same but different too.

Psalm 139 is a wonderful chapter of the Bible that talks about how well God knows you. Read this psalm now with your family.

Your Outside

Now, let's talk about verses 13-14: "You made my whole being. You formed me in my mother's body. I praise you because you made me in an amazing and wonderful way." Take a moment to look at your hands, your feet, your arms, and your legs. Do you have any special marks or scars, anything that makes you unique or different? Look very carefully at your fingerprints—the patterns of tiny lines on your fingers.

This verse is telling you that God specifically designed those fingerprints *just for you*. And not only did He make every part of you, this psalm says that He did it in an amazing and wonderful way!

Your Inside

God not only created the outside of your body to make you special and unique, He created your inside too. God gave you your own personality, your own likes and dislikes, your own strengths and weaknesses. He knew the things you would be interested in, and He knew what would make you smile. According to Psalm 139:4, He even knows the words you are going to say before they come out of your mouth!

In Luke 12, Jesus was telling His followers how well He knew them. He said, "God even knows how many hairs you have on your head" (v. 7). How could that be? Think of all the little hairs attached to your head. God knows the number of hairs? Yes, He does! He knows you inside and out, and He made you just the way you are.

Praying This Week:

Praise God for the way that He made you. Think of a different way each day, and praise Him for it. You might say, "I praise You for making me run fast." Or, "I praise You for making me love to laugh!" Tell Him how creative and loving He is.

Lord, You are perfect!
I praise You for all the
ways You are wonderful.

Who You Are

Take your prayer journal and write down everything you know about who God is. Make a list with your family and see how many character traits you can come up with.

Now, read the list below. Pick out a few of your favorite ones, and read the verses:

- *God does not change:* Hebrews 13:8
- *God is patient:* 2 Peter 3:9
- *God is light:* Psalm 27:1
- *God never gets tired:* Isaiah 40:28
- *God is a shield:* Psalm 18:30
- *God is forgiving:* Psalm 103:3
- *God is love:* 1 John 4:8
- *God is the way, truth, and life:* John 14:6
- *God is your helper:* John 14:26
- *God is a giver:* John 3:16; James 1:17
- *God is creative:* Job 12:7–10
- *God is perfect:* Matthew 5:48

We could go on all day looking at verses that tell us more about who our amazing God is!

Galatians 5:22–23 tells us that people who are guided by God's Spirit will be like Him: they will have *love, joy, peace, patience, kindness, goodness, faithfulness, gentleness,* and *self-control.* Many parts of the Bible tell us that God is *holy.* Do you know what that means? It means He is perfectly good. To be holy is to be pure and clean, thinking good thoughts and doing good things.

More About God . . .

God is also *compassionate,* and full of *grace* and *mercy* (giving us what we don't deserve, and *not* giving us the bad things we do deserve!). He is our *friend,* He is *true,* and He is *right.* One other wonderful trait of God is that He is *faithful.* That means no matter what happens, God will always be there. Nothing can cause Him to give up on you. *Nothing.*

Praying This Week:

There are so many reasons to praise God's character! Pick your favorite thing about who God is, and draw a picture of what you think that looks like in your prayer journal. Keep the list you made in your journal by your bed, and talk to God about all of His wonderful traits. He knows all about who He is, but He loves to hear you say it.

Jesus, I mess up a lot!
I need to tell You about
what I have done wrong.

Week 24

Confession

Use some washable markers to give each person in your family a dot on the tip of their nose. Be sure not to let them see what color you use. Now, have someone put a dot on the tip of your nose without your knowing the color either. This may look a little funny! Can you see the color on your nose? Can you guess what it is? Take turns letting everyone guess what color is on their own nose.

We All Sin

I am sure you have heard of the word *sin*. A *sin* is anything you do that is wrong in God's eyes. Many times, just like with the marker dots, it is much easier to see someone else's sin than it is to see our own. We often don't think we are doing anything wrong, when really, we are. Here is a list of some sins we struggle with: lying, cheating, being disobedient, being unkind, using mean words, disrespecting grown-ups, having a bad attitude, looking at things we shouldn't, thinking thoughts that are not right, and worrying too much. God knows we are not perfect, but when we act like this, we are actually sinning *against* Him.

First John 1:9 says, "If we confess our sins, he will forgive our sins. . . . He will make us clean from all the wrongs we have done." We need God to help us see our sin. Can you ask Him for His help?

Telling God

Does 1 John 1:9 say that we can sin and then God will automatically forgive us? No, look closer. Is there something that we need to do before God forgives us? What is it? We have to confess our sins to God. *Confession* is a fancy word that means telling someone something. To confess our sins means to tell God about the things we have done wrong. Even though God already knows that you have sinned, it is important for you to tell Him about it. It may sound something like this: "Lord, yesterday I pushed my sister because I was angry. I am sorry for pushing her. Please forgive me." That is confessing your sin to God.

Praying This Week:

Every day, take your prayer journal and write down one thing you need to confess to God. If you can't think of anything, pray for a little bit, then try again. He promises to hear you and, even better, to forgive you.

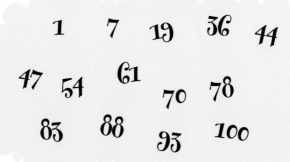

Father, please forgive me for thinking things that are not pleasing to You. Show me the thoughts I need to confess today.

Sins I've Thought

In your head, pick a number between one and one hundred. Have each family member guess a number, and answer their guesses only by saying "too high" or "too low." Do this until they finally guess the right number. Then give someone else a turn. After you have played a few times, talk about this: Did you like being the only one to know the number? When you are thinking something that no one else knows about, is that a good thing or a bad thing? Is it possible to have a thought that God does not know about?

Sometimes it seems that just *thinking* sinful thoughts is not wrong as long as we are not *doing* anything. That's not true. It might not be easy to notice, but we can teach ourselves to pay attention to those times our thoughts don't please God and confess those sinful thoughts to Him.

Watch Out!

Second Corinthians 10:5 tells us that we can "capture" our thoughts: "We capture every thought and make it give up and obey Christ." How in the world can you

111

capture a thought? If you are going to capture something, like a fly, you have to do two things: You have to be watching closely, and you have to be quick! Capturing our thoughts just means being careful and aware of what we are thinking, and then quickly saying, "Oops, that thought was a sin!" For instance, if you are getting very frustrated at your mom or dad for asking you to do something you don't want to do, you might start thinking things like: *I don't like her. I want to punch him. She doesn't love me.* In that moment, seeing that you have sinned and then confessing it to God is capturing that thought so that He can help you get rid of it.

Thinking and Doing

In Matthew 5, Jesus taught us all about sinful thoughts. In fact, He even said that *thinking* something sinful is

not all that different from *doing* something sinful. So if you were to think about hurting someone you were angry with, Jesus said it's just as if you did hurt them. Your thoughts matter to God.

Praying This Week:

Pay special attention to your thoughts. Try to catch yourself thinking something you shouldn't and, right then and there, confess it to God. Use your journal to tell God about things you may need to stop thinking about. Remember, He already knows all your thoughts, and He is waiting and ready to forgive you and help you.

SIN =  >

**Jesus, I confess
to You the things
I have done
wrong today.**

Sins I've Acted On

Draw a picture in your journal of three things: a hand, a heart, and a head. Where does sin start? Where does it end? See if you can number those three things in the right order.

We have talked about how we need to confess sins that are only in our minds. When we do that, we keep ourselves from taking our sin to the next step: actually *doing* something wrong. James 1:14–15 tells us that the evil we sometimes want to do can lead us away from God and eventually cause us to sin.

Are there sins you have thought but not confessed to God? If so, you might act out on those sins before you even know it. Our heart is the part of us that loves and wants things. If we stop putting God first, our hearts drift away from Him, and we start to love other things more. Sin starts in our hearts, then moves to our thoughts (heads), then ends with our actions (hands).

Jealous Brothers

Do you know the story of Joseph? You can read all about him in Genesis 37–50. Joseph was Jacob's favorite son. All his brothers were very jealous of him because their father loved him the most. One day his brothers had a thought: *Let's sell Joseph as a slave in Egypt and tell our father that he has died. That's what he gets for being the favorite!* Instead of confessing that thought to God, they did what they had planned to do, and they sold Joseph as a slave.

That one decision caused many people a lot of hurt and confusion. When we sin, we are not the only people who feel consequences of that sin. A *consequence* is something that happens because of an action that was taken. The sin of Joseph's brothers caused sad, difficult things to happen to Joseph, Jacob, and many others.

Your Actions

Can you think of a sin you have acted on, and someone else who suffered because of it? Since we are closest to our families and we are with them the most often, they are usually the people we hurt most by our sins. You may be having a hard time obeying a parent, or you may be fighting a lot with a brother or sister. Is there something you need to confess to your family and to God today?

Praying This Week:

Think about sins you have acted on, and write a letter to someone who suffered because of your sin. Tell them you are sorry that your sin caused them to be hurt or sad, and ask for forgiveness. Tell God about the sins you have acted on, and be sure to remember that once you confess a sin—as quick as lightning—it is forgiven.

Lord, there are some things
You have told me to do, and I
have not done what You asked.
I confess those things today.

Things I Should Have Done

Find a rope or anything you can use for tug-of-war. Play a few rounds of the game with someone, and then try this: Just hold the rope while the other person pulls. What happened when you didn't pull on it yourself? You lost the rope! Sometimes *doing nothing* is the same as doing something wrong.

Just Do It!

James 4:17 says that "when a person knows the right thing to do, but does not do it, then he is sinning." We don't only sin against God when we are acting on our sins; we also sin against Him when we are *not* acting on what He has told us to do. It's sort of like your basketball coach telling you to pass the ball, but instead, you just stand there. Or like your teacher asking you to get your pencil, but instead, you just sit at your desk, staring at her.

The Good Samaritan

Jesus showed us exactly what this means in His story about the good Samaritan found in Luke 10. A man was traveling on the road when he was attacked and beaten by robbers. They tore off his clothes and left him lying in the road, almost dead. A Jewish priest was walking down the same road, and when he saw the man, he went over to the other side of the road and walked right past him. Next, another man called a Levite came by, went over to the man and looked at him, then kept on walking. Then finally, a Samaritan man came walking down that same road. He saw the man and felt sorry for him. But instead of passing by and doing nothing, he put medicine and bandages on all his wounds, put him on his donkey, and took him to an inn. At the inn, the Samaritan took care of the man and paid the innkeeper to do the same until he was feeling better.

Which of these men did the right thing? Even though the first two men did not do anything evil,

they decided *not* to do good to someone who needed help. Galatians 6:9 says, "We must not become tired of doing good." When we see something good to do, we should always do it!

Praying This Week:

What are some things God has told you to do? Here are a few: love others (John 13:34), serve others (Mark 9:35), read His Word (Joshua 1:8), and help those in need (Hebrew 13:16). Spend some time being quiet with God, and pray that He will point out to you those things He is asking you to do that you are not doing. Confess that to Him in prayer, and, as always, thank Him for His forgiveness.

Father, there are some things I just can't stop doing. You are stronger than I am, and I know You can help.

Sins I Keep Doing

Try to tell your family a story without using the word *and*. Then have someone else tell a story without saying the word *the*. Talk about this: Was it hard not to say that certain word? Did you keep messing up and saying it anyway? Sometimes sin can be like that too.

When It's Hard to Stop

Have you ever felt like it was too hard to stop doing certain things? Maybe you really want to do better, and you have confessed your sin to God, but you just keep doing the wrong thing. Even Paul, a man who did incredible things for Jesus and who spread His Word all over the world, felt this way. He said, "I do not understand the things I do. I do not do the good things I want to do. And I do the bad things I hate to do" (Romans 7:15). Then he said this: "So if I do things I do not want to do, then I am not the one doing those things. It is sin living in me that does those bad things" (Romans 7:20).

Paul was saying that because of what happened

all those years ago in the garden with Adam and Eve, we all have sin in us. And although Jesus came to die for that sin and we are saved from it, we still have to fight against it every day. Once we understand that we can't stop sinning as long as we're only using our own strength, God can help us. Philippians 2:13 says, "God is working in you to help you want to do what pleases him. Then he gives you the power to do it." You can't do it without Him!

Asking for Help

Spend some time with your family talking about a sin that you seem to keep doing over and over again. It might feel weird saying it out loud, but remember that God gave us a family so we could talk and help each other through this crazy life. After you have talked about your sins, spend some time together praying for each other. Ask God to remind each of you that only He has the power to help you. Tell Him you need Him and you want His help.

Praying This Week:

Think about one particular sin that you need help getting rid of. Remember, don't try to stop on your own! You need God to do it through you. Talk to God about your struggle with this sin, and ask Him for help.

Father, teach me to put on my armor and fight against the things that are tempting me.

Sins That Are Calling Me

If you have a pet, put it in the room with you. If you don't have a pet, have one person in the family pretend to be one! Have everyone sit in a different spot of the room and call your pet over to them. You can say or do silly things to get your pet to come to you. Then talk about why the pet went to that certain person.

This seems crazy, but just as you were calling the pet, sometimes sin can call your name. We call this *temptation*. Temptation is when we really want to do something we know is wrong. We are "tempted" when we are trying to decide whether to do something we know we shouldn't. What are some things that tempt you? Talk about that with your family.

God's Armor

Everyone is tempted. But the good thing is, God promises in 1 Corinthians 10:13 that He will not let us be tempted more than we can handle and that He will help us find a way out. Fighting against temptation is kind of like fighting in a war. If you don't wear any

127

armor to protect you, you will certainly die! Would you ever go out onto a battlefield without any weapons or anything to guard your body? No! Neither should you go out into the world and fight all your temptations without God's armor strapped on tight.

Read Ephesians 6:10–20 with your family. Talk about what each piece of armor represents:

- Belt
- Breastplate
- Shoes
- Shield
- Helmet
- Sword

And what is the last thing (maybe the most important) this passage tells us to do in order to fight against temptations and win? Well, of course . . . *pray!*

Praying This Week:

List your biggest temptations in your prayer journal. Confess to God the times you have given in to temptation, and tell Him you need His help to resist it. Be watching and listening for when temptation calls your name. When it does, right then and there, talk to God about it. Oh, and have your armor on and ready to use!

Jesus, thank You
for Your mercy! As
I confess my sins to
You today, I remember
Your promises to me.

A Hundred Chances

Find a paper plate and a container of salt. With a parent's help, pour a large amount of salt on the plate and spread it around the plate. Then, with your finger, write the word *sin* in the salt. Can you see the word? Now take the plate and gently shake or move the salt all around (without spilling any!) so the word disappears. When we confess our sins to God, that is what happens. Those sins disappear—just like that—*forever!*

Mercy for Jonah

Time and time again in the Bible, God has mercy on people who mess up. *Mercy* is being kind to people who don't deserve it, or giving help to people who are in a bad situation. Remember the story of Jonah? After Jonah disobeyed and ran from God, he was thrown into the sea, swallowed by a fish, and spit out on dry land. What happened next? God offered Jonah another chance, and Jonah took it! He went to Nineveh to do what God had first asked him to do.

There is a passage in the Bible that tells us that

God offers us a chance to start over and turn from our sins every single day. It's Lamentations 3:21–23, and it says: "I have hope when I think of this: The Lord's love never ends. His mercies never stop. They are new every morning." God does not just give us one more chance . . . He gives us one hundred more chances! And then some more! We are so blessed to have a Father who gives us mercy every day.

Mercy for Others

Is there someone in your life who could use some mercy? This could be someone who has done something wrong or is having a hard day. It could be someone who is in trouble or has even done or said something mean to you. For example, if your friend says something to hurt you, giving mercy would be saying something back that is kind or loving . . . even though your friend may not deserve it. Giving mercy shows others who God is. Ask the Lord if there is someone He wants you to show His mercy to today.

Praying This Week:

As you continue focusing on confessing your sins to God in your journal, remember God's promise to erase your sin and give you another chance. When you first see sunlight coming through your window in the morning, let it remind you that God has given you a new day and a brand-new start. And then say, "Thank You, God!"

Father, You have forgiven me
for so much! Now help
me to forgive others.

Forgiving Like God

Play a game of Simon Says with your family. Let each person take a turn being "Simon" while everyone else copies what Simon says to do. Then talk about this: Was it hard or easy to copy someone else? Did you like having others copy you? Is there someone in your life that you want to copy or imitate like that?

Fully and Freely

We have talked a lot about how God forgives us . . . fully (all the way) and freely (He gives it to us for nothing). God shows us forgiveness because He loves us, but also because He wants us to forgive others. He is the example that we are to follow—what He does, we need to do ourselves. If you are copying God by forgiving, then others will copy you, and everyone will be doing what God says works best.

In Mark 11:25, Jesus said to His disciples, "When you are praying, and you remember that you are angry with another person about something, then forgive him. If you do this, then your Father in heaven will also forgive your sins." So if you're praying and you realize that you have anger or unforgiveness in your heart toward someone, Jesus says you need to deal with that right away. You might think, *But I am so mad at him! How can I forgive him when he makes me this angry?*

It's Up to You

Sometimes it helps to stay away from that person for a little while and just be quiet. You can tell God that you are mad—since, remember, He is *always* listening! And most importantly, you can ask the Holy Spirit of God who lives inside you to help you forgive. Then you just have to make the choice to do it.

You see, God does not force us to forgive others. He tells us to, but it's up to us to choose to do it. God knows it is always best for you to forgive, especially since you have Someone forgiving you every day!

Praying This Week:

You have now been confessing your sins to God for a few weeks. Think about all the sins you have confessed and all the things for which God has forgiven you. He is such a wonderful, loving, merciful Father. Tell Him that this week. Remember all the forgiveness that has fallen on you like rain, and ask Him to show you who you can forgive as you follow His example.

Jesus, I want to talk to You
about someone in my family
who needs You today.

Week 32

Help for My Family

What do you love most about your family? Have each person answer these questions: What is your favorite family memory? What are some funny things that have happened in our family? What is the hardest thing we have ever been through as a family?

Where to Go

Sometimes we pray because someone we know needs help. The book of Psalms is full of prayers from people crying out for help. Where do you go when you need help? What about the times when you are really sad, and you just don't see how things are going to get better? Where do you go then? Psalm 121:1–2 says, "I look up to the hills. But where does my help come from? My help comes from the Lord. He made heaven and earth." Of course! You go to the Maker of heaven and earth, the One who says His thoughts about you are more than the number of grains of sand (Psalm 139:17–18)!

Your Team

When we were learning to pray with thankful hearts, we talked about our families. God gave you a family so you would have people to be with in life. He said it wasn't good for man to be alone, and so He made the family. Your family can be there for you; they're kind of like your "team." You are together, and no one should ever come between you.

Just as your family can be there for you when you need them, you can be there for them when they need you. And one of the best ways to do that is to pray for them. Is anyone in your family sick? Is anyone in your family going through a hard time? You might want to stop and pray for them now, and remind them that their help comes from the Lord.

Praying This Week:

Make a Family Prayer List. Have each person say something they would like you to pray for, and write that something down next to their name. Each day, pick one person and talk about them to God. Tell Him what they need, and ask Him for His help. If you run out of people during the week, just start over! Think of yourself as holding them up as you bring them to Jesus. Your help comes from Him!

Lord, I want to pray for others. Show me a friend who needs Your help today.

Help for My Friends

Here's a challenge for you: Have your family stand behind you in two rows, facing each other and locking arms—creating a sort of net. Then, as you are standing up straight, fall backward into their locked arms without bending your knees. (Make sure a parent is helping!) You might be scared at first, but try to trust that they are back there and they will not let you fall! Take turns having other family members do the same.

Help Each Other Up

Just as God gave us a family so that we would not be alone, He has given us friends so that we can help each other when life gets hard. Like your family members kept you from falling, you and your friends can hold each other up by praying for each other. The Bible says this: "Two people are better than one. They get more done by working together. If one person falls, the other can help him up" (Ecclesiastes 4:9–10). When we pray, it's important to think of other people and not only ourselves. We can talk to God about our friends.

The Golden Rule

When you hear the word *friend*, what do you think about? Tell your family your answer. You could talk about characteristics of a good friend or about some of your closest friends and why you like them. Jesus talked about why it is important to care about our friends. He told us in Luke 10:27 that we are to love our neighbors the same way that we love ourselves. This is what we call the golden rule. It means that if you have a friend who is having a hard time, you should do for them what you would want someone to do for you. If you were feeling alone, you would want someone to talk to you. If you were having a hard time with school, you would want someone to help you. Your friends might need the same thing from you!

Jesus wants us to care about others and to pray for people who are hurting or having problems. Do you have a friend who is sometimes sad? Do you know anyone who has health problems? Have you ever seen someone who is bullied or picked on? You can pray for these friends and ask God to help them.

Praying This Week:

Think of two friends you can pray for. Write their names in your journal, and talk to God about each of them at different times of the week. You might want to write one of them a note and include Psalm 121 as a reminder that their help comes from God.

Jesus, I pray for all those in Your family who are suffering. I ask You to give them strength.

Week 34

Help for the Church

What is *the church*, and how did it become what it is?
See what everyone in your family thinks.

God's Family

In the Bible, the church is not described as a build-
ing, but as *a group of people*. After Jesus died and
went up into heaven, His followers devoted their lives
to loving Him and telling others about Him. They
stayed together, shared all they had with each other,
and watched God do amazing miracles (Acts 2). This
is how the church came to be. After a short time, they
moved into different parts of the world, spreading
the news of Jesus. And thanks to them, you know Him
today, and you are a part of His church.

So if we are a part of the church (Christians all over
the world), we are all a part of each other. We are a
family—God's family. When someone in your family is
hurt or sad, do you pray for them? In the same way,
if someone in God's family is having troubles, we can
pray for them too.

When the Church Suffers

Some of these Christians live in places that can be scary—countries where you are not allowed to believe in God or even talk to Him. Some of these people are put in jail or even killed for saying that they are Christians. Think about how you would feel if that happened in *your* country, in *your* family. Let's be thankful that we live in a place where we are free to worship God anytime we want. And let's be praying for all the people in God's church who suffer and who are punished for simply believing in God. *They need our prayers!*

Even though it's hard to understand why this happens, we must remember what God said in Deuteronomy 31:6: "Be strong and brave. Don't be afraid of them. Don't be frightened. The Lord your God will go with you. He will not leave you or forget you."

Praying This Week:

Spend some time each day praying for the church all around the world. Pray for the kids who are scared or confused. Ask God to help the men and women to be brave and strong and to have faith in Him. Pray for the Holy Spirit to give peace to each of them and to be their help in times of trouble. Then pray for your local church—the group of people you worship with every week. Pray that God would protect your pastor and the other leaders in your church. Pray that they would be bold and bring many people to Jesus.

Note to parents: For further exploration of this subject, visit the website of Voice of the Martyrs, www.persecution.com, and their website for children, www.kidsofcourage.com.

Jesus, I pray for all
the children who are
hungry and sick.
Please show them
Your love today.

Help for the Hungry

Pass out one cracker, or about a fourth of a piece of bread, to each person in your family. As you begin, have everyone eat their portion and talk about what it would be like if that were all you had to eat, all day, every day.

Hunger in the World

In the world today, there are about 800 million hungry people (www.worldhunger.org). That is a really large number, right? Many of those people are children, just like you. These families are very poor, and their parents do not have enough money to buy food. In some places there is not much food and water, which means everyone who lives there goes hungry. Since these children don't eat enough, they get sick and sometimes are too weak even to walk or play outside. Some things in the world are hard to understand, and this is one of them. But God understands. He sees each one of those children, and He knows each one by name.

151

Sometimes we might feel helpless, thinking about all the hungry people in the world and wondering what we can do to help. One way is to pray for them! God knows who they are, so you can ask Him to show His love to them in some way. Ask Him to provide for a hungry little girl tonight, or ask Him to heal a sick little boy.

You Can Help

Another thing you can do is give! Proverbs 28:27 says, "The person who gives to the poor will have every-thing he needs." There are many organizations that help people who are poor and hungry. You can give some of your money to help them, and sometimes you can even see a picture of the child you are help-ing! You may write a letter to that child and then hear about how your help is giving them what they need.

Praying This Week:

Have your parent help you think of a country in which many poor, hungry people live. Spend some time praying for the children there. Pray that they would come to know about God's love for them and know that He is with them. Pray that God would provide help and food for them. And every time you pray before a meal, remember all that you have with a grateful heart.

Note to parents: For further exploration of this subject, visit www.fh.org or www.compassion.com.

God, I pray for the people
who don't know about
Your wonderful love.
Help me to show it to them.

Help for the Lost

In a room with a closed door, close your eyes and have someone spin you around ten times. Then try to find your way to the door without any help. Did you feel confused? Did you need help to find your way?

A Reason and a Purpose

Several times in the Bible, we see the phrase "the lost." What do you think that means? When you know God, you have a reason for living. You have a plan to follow (His Word!), and you have a purpose for being here. Your reason for living is to learn how to love God and to show His love to others. Your plan is to obey what He has told you to do in His Word, until one day He brings you home with Him. But people who do not know or follow God do not have the same purpose or plan for their lives. They don't know the way to go in this world because they are "lost" without God.

Luke 19:10 says, "The Son of Man came to find lost people and save them." That was Jesus' whole reason for coming to earth! His purpose was to find people who were lost and to save them from their sins.

Lost and Found

In Romans 10:1–2, the apostle Paul prayed for all the people who were lost and didn't know God. He said he wanted them to be saved more than he wanted anything else. Like Paul, we can pray for people who we know are lost and do not know Jesus. We can ask God to make their hearts listen to His voice, to help them turn around and follow Him. We can pray that they will start to understand how deep and wide His love is!

Stop and read the story of the lost sheep in Matthew 18:12–14 with your family. Then answer these questions: Why did the shepherd leave his ninety-nine sheep? What made him happy? Who is just like the shepherd? Does God really care about the lost?

Praying This Week:

Think of someone you know who may not know God. Pray for that person by name every day. Ask God to give you a chance to tell them about His love or to invite them to church. Be looking for those chances, and keep praying as you go!

Father, I pray for my country
and its leaders. Show them
Your power and might.

Help for Our Country

Find a piece of poster board, a white pillowcase, or a large sheet of white paper. Decorate what you found by making it into your country's flag. Have everyone participate, then hang it up in the room and sing a song about your country.

Our Leaders

The Bible says, "You should pray for kings and for all who have authority. Pray for the leaders so that we can have quiet and peaceful lives—lives full of worship and respect for God" (1 Timothy 2:2). As followers of Jesus, we are asked to pray for the people who make decisions for our country. Sometimes we agree with our leaders; sometimes we do not. But the Bible actually tells us in Romans 13:1 that no one has any power or position that God has not allowed them to have. He is always in control! So no matter what you think about your leaders, the right thing to do is to pray for them.

How exactly should we pray for our president and leaders?

- Pray they would know and follow God.
- Pray they would be protected from anything evil.
- Pray for their families.
- Pray for wisdom in every decision.

God's Word also says to pray for our country. God has placed you right where you are for a reason, and you should have a love and respect for your "home"— your country.

A Great Land

Solomon was King David's son. The Lord was with Solomon and made him into a great, powerful king. God told Solomon in 2 Chronicles 7:14 that He wanted His people to be sorry for the wrong things they had done, to pray to Him and obey Him, and to turn away from evil. He said if they did those things, He would hear their prayers, forgive them, and make their land great again. We should pray that our country would do those things too.

Praying This Week:

In your prayer journal, write down three things that you love about your country and three things you wish were different. Then write down a few names of the leaders of your country. Pray for them by name, and ask God for His blessing on your homeland.

God, please make me wise! Give me understanding, and help me.

Wisdom from Above

Stand on the opposite side of the room from your parent, and then have them ask you each a question about the Bible. If you get it right, you can take one giant step forward. If you get it wrong, take a giant step back. Whoever gets to the other side first is the winner! (If you don't have any brothers or sisters, see how many steps it takes you to get there!)

Being Wise

Being wise can help you get places in your life. But having wisdom is more than just being smart or getting the right answer on a test. Wisdom is knowing how to tell if something is good or bad—and making choices that are right and smart. Proverbs 2:6 says, "Only the Lord gives wisdom. Knowledge and understanding come from him." Over and over, God tells us to ask Him to make us wise.

Wisdom is like a great treasure. Proverbs 8:11 says, "Wisdom is more precious than rubies. Nothing you want is equal to it." This means that nothing else you will find or want will be as good for you as wisdom is. For example, without wisdom, you might talk too much and your words could hurt others. But with wisdom, you would know when to be quiet and what to say at the right time. Wisdom can also keep you from making choices that will not turn out well for you.

Read the following passages with your family, and then talk about each one and how God uses things in our lives to give us wisdom from above: Proverbs 1:8; 4:20, 26–27.

The Best Request

Those are only some of the ways in which you can become wise. The book of Proverbs is full of them! God loves for us to ask for wisdom. In fact, one day God told King Solomon to ask for anything he wanted—*anything*. He could have asked for more money to buy more things, or more power to rule over more people, or a long, long life. But can you guess what he asked

for instead? Yes—wisdom from God! He wanted God to make him wise and to help him make good decisions for his people. God told Solomon this was the best thing he could have asked for. Then He answered his prayer.

Praying This Week:

Spend some time in the book of Proverbs. Start with Proverbs 1, and pay close attention every time you see the word *wise* or *wisdom*. Ask God to help you become wise and to make good choices. Remember that nothing you could ever want is as good for you as wisdom from above.

God, help me to take
a break from thinking
and doing, and just sit
still and be with You.

Week 39

Being Still

Have someone in your family whisper a long, made-up sentence in your ear while you are wriggling all around or jumping up and down. Then have them whisper a new sentence to you while you are sitting completely still and quiet. Which sentence could you hear the best? Which one could you remember the most? Why do you think that is?

The First Step

We have learned a lot about how to talk to God—how to thank Him, praise Him, confess to Him, and ask Him for all kinds of help. But there is much more to praying than just talking to God . . . that is only half of it! If you had a friend who talked to you all the time and never stopped to listen to what *you* had to say, how would you feel? If we want to be close to God, we have to learn how to listen to His voice. And the first step to hearing God's voice is being still.

Calm and Quiet

In Psalm 46:10, God said, "Be quiet and know that I am God" (NLV). Being still and quiet before God helps us to hear Him. It takes away things that distract us. Sometimes we get so busy doing things we think are important that we are never still long enough to hear God speak to us. Being still and quiet actually takes practice!

Having some times of quiet can be very good for you and for your heart. Psalm 131:2 says, "I am calm and quiet. . . . I am at peace, like a baby with its mother." God loves for us to come to Him, calm and quiet, listening for His voice.

Praying This Week:

After you finish praying, practice being totally still and quiet for three minutes. Make sure you are in a quiet place by yourself. You might think about things that happened that day, or you might think about God and what He is doing in your life right now. Try to stop your mind from wandering, and keep thinking about Him. I think you will like it!

Jesus, I want to know and to hear Your voice. Speak to me today. I am listening.

A Whispering Voice

How well do you know the voices in your family? Close your eyes tight, and then have each person in your family take turns whispering something in your ear while you try to guess who is whispering to you. Were your guesses right or wrong?

When God Speaks

In Bible times, God spoke to His people in many ways. In the book of Job, He spoke through a whirlwind, in Exodus through a cloud, and in Psalms in a voice like thunder. Today, God's voice is usually small and quiet. He doesn't talk to us in a normal voice, or through a burning bush like He did with Moses. God talks to us softly. We can't really hear these whispers with our ears, but we can hear them in our hearts.

The Holy Spirit, who lives inside you, tells your heart what is right and true, and what God wants you to know. As you get older, you will be able to tell when He is speaking to you and what He is saying to your heart. Sometimes you might think, *I shouldn't do this.*

That is God speaking to your heart. Other times you might think, *Wow, I feel like God loves me a lot!* That is God telling you that!

How God Speaks

God speaks to us in a few different ways. Can you think of any? He speaks to us through His Word, the Bible (every word is absolutely true!); He can speak to us through other people (like pastors or teachers); and He can speak to us with His quiet whisper.

Jesus said, "My sheep listen to my voice. I know them, and they follow me. I give them eternal life, and they will never die. And no person can steal them out of my hand" (John 10:27–28). He was saying that if we belong to Him, we will learn to recognize His voice.

Have you ever heard Jesus say something to you? What was it? Talk about that with your family.

Praying This Week:

Spend some time trying to hear God speak to you. One day, read a chapter in your Bible, and write in your prayer journal what you think God is saying. Another day, listen to a teacher or parent, and write something down in your journal about that too. Last, take a day just to be still and quiet, and see if God says anything in your heart. Remember, God whispers, so listen closely!

Shhh...

Father, I know You are there
even when I can't hear You.
Give me faith to believe!

When I Can't Hear You

Play the "Silent Game." Whoever talks or makes a noise first is out! Then talk about this: Was it hard to stay silent? What do you like better: talking or being quiet?

Trusting When It's Quiet

There will be times in your life when you really want God to speak to you. You will come to Him, you will be still and quiet, and yet you will not hear Him speak. Job was a man in the Bible who suffered a lot. As all kinds of bad things were happening to him, he was going to God and asking for help. But God seemed silent. For the first 37 chapters of Job, God was quiet. Throughout that time Job knew that God was there and that He was in control of everything. He trusted that God would do what was best in his life, even if he couldn't hear Him.

You might think, *Why would God want to stay silent? Why won't He answer my prayer?* One reason could be that He is trying to teach you something. Maybe He wants to help you understand a part of His character in a new way. No matter what happens, He wants you to keep seeking Him, and that may mean you have to trust that He is being quiet for a good reason.

Too Busy

Many times, we do not hear God speak simply because we are too busy. Do you remember the story of Mary and Martha? When Jesus came to their house, Martha was working hard on all her chores while Mary was sitting at the feet of Jesus, listening. Jesus told them that Mary had chosen the right thing—being still and listening. Martha was too busy with other things to hear God speak to her.

Other times, God is quiet because we have sins that we need to confess to Him. Maybe there is someone you need to apologize to, or something you did that you need to make right. God might be waiting for you to confess your sin before He speaks to you.

Praying This Week:

Continue being still and quiet—this time for five minutes every day. Confess your sins to God and keep asking Him to speak to you. Write down in your prayer journal anything you think He is saying to you. He may speak through His Word, through other people, or to your heart as you are being still. Remember, we have to learn how to listen . . . it does not come easily for us! When God seems quiet, tell Him that you trust Him and that you know He hears your prayers.

Lord, thank You for speaking to me through all the things Your hands have made. Help me to hear You.

Your Creation

Have you ever seen the ocean? Have you ever watched an awesome sunset or stood on a mountain, feeling a cool breeze? Maybe you like hearing birds sing or watching ants in a line, working for their food. Tell your family your favorite thing about nature. And if there is any part of God's creation that makes you feel close to Him, tell them that too.

Nature Speaks

God speaks to us through His creation. Just by looking at the beautiful things He has made and seeing how He has put the earth in motion, we can hear God speak. What is He communicating? He is showing us that He is *amazing*. He is saying that He sees us. And He is making it clear that He is in control of everything.

Psalm 19:1–4 says, "The heavens tell the glory of God. And the skies announce what his hands have made. Day after day they tell the story. Night after night they tell it again. They have no speech or words. They don't make any sound to be heard. But their message goes out through all the world. It goes everywhere on earth."

Sometimes it's good to spend time talking to God as you are lying in the grass, looking up at the sky. You can talk to Him on a walk, on your bike, or on a swing. Being outside in God's creation can make it seem like we are closer to Him. We are closer to the things His hands have made, focused on His creation and not so distracted by the things we have inside.

Learning from Creation

Jesus taught a lot of lessons using things in nature. In Matthew 6, Jesus was teaching His disciples not to worry so much. He told them to look at the birds in the sky. The birds don't plant or store food, but God makes sure they are fed. He also said to look at the flowers in the field. Those flowers don't make their

own clothes—but look how beautiful they are, because God made them that way! So you see, if God takes care of birds and flowers, don't you think He will take care of *you*? You can learn a lot from looking at the things God's hands have made.

Praying This Week:

Try to spend five minutes every day outside, by yourself, talking to God. Tell Him about your day and what is on your mind. Then spend a few minutes just being quiet and looking at all the things He has made. Watch and listen . . . you just might hear Him speak!

God, I want to hear
You speak to me
through Your Word!
I know it is for me.

Your Word Is for Me

What is your favorite verse from the Bible? Have each family member share theirs, and then talk about what you think God is saying in each verse. Is He speaking? Can you hear Him?

A Story of Love

The main way Jesus speaks to us today is through His Word—the Bible. You probably remember that the Bible was written by many different authors. These people were all chosen by God to tell the story of His love for us. You can even think of God's Word as His "love letter" to you. Throughout the Bible, God tells us how to live and reminds us that He is always there and always loving us. If you are having a hard time listening to God, spend some time reading your Bible—it was written for you!

What's the Big Deal?

There may be times in your life when you get tired of people telling you to read the Bible. Maybe you have heard that a lot. You might think, *What is the big deal?* The apostle Paul answered that question for you in 2 Timothy 3:14–17 when he said:

> You should continue following the teachings that you learned. You know that these teachings are true. And you know that you can trust those who taught you. You have known the Holy Scriptures since you were a child. The Scriptures are able to make you wise. And that wisdom leads to salvation through faith in Christ Jesus. All Scripture is inspired by God and is useful for teaching and for showing people what is wrong in their lives. It is useful for correcting faults and teaching how to live right. Using the Scriptures, the person who serves God will be ready and will have everything he needs to do every good work.

What great reasons to pay attention to God's Word!

Praying This Week:

Keep your Bible with you each day while you pray. Pick a book of the Bible—like John, Matthew, Psalms, or Proverbs—and read one chapter every day. After you read it, write down in your journal anything you think God is saying to you. Listen closely to what He says. And then write a love letter back to Him!

DEAR GOD...

Jesus, help me listen
to the people You have
put in my life. Thank
You for speaking to
me through others.

People Talking

Pretend for a moment that you are a soldier, hiding out in a fort, and the enemy is approaching. You need to hear from your commander because you don't know where you should go next. All of a sudden, you see a messenger! Someone is running toward your fort to tell you what the commander has said to do. Are you glad he is there? Are you listening? In the same way, God sends us "messengers" to show us the way to live.

Messengers

We have talked a lot about how God speaks and how we can listen. We know that God speaks to us through His small, quiet voice in our hearts, through His Word, and through creation. There is one more way God can speak to us, and that is through other people. God has put parents, grandparents, teachers, and others in your life so that you will have people to help you know the way to go. They hear things from God, and then tell those things to you. It's a little bit like your mom asking you to tell your little brother that it is time for dinner. She is using you to give him a message from her. The same is true for the people in our lives who teach us about God.

Be Wise and Listen!

Proverbs 12:15 says, "A foolish person thinks he is doing right. But a wise person listens to advice." This means that we are smart and wise if we listen to what our parents and teachers say to us. You see, the people God sends your way have lived longer than you, and they know things that you have not yet learned. Maybe your mom or dad did something as a child that did not work out very well. They might want to tell you, "Wait! Don't do it that way; do it *this* way. Trust me, I know!" You are very wise to listen to that advice and to realize that it is God showing you the way to go.

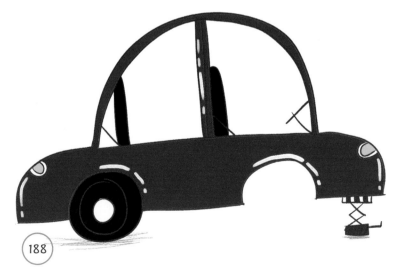

Praying This Week:

Whenever you're with the people in your life who teach you about God, try to give them your full attention. Listen to what they say, and see if you can hear God say anything to you through them. Write one of those people a note, thanking them for being God's messenger to you.

Lord, thank You for
showing me how
important it is to pray.
You are my example.

Week 45

Jesus Prayed

Find a picture of your favorite animal and look at it for ten seconds. Then put it away and try to draw it. Now try drawing it one more time, but this time with the picture right in front of you. How different were the pictures you drew? I bet your second drawing turned out more like your example!

Just like you would copy or imitate that picture, you can copy and imitate the things that Jesus did while He was on earth—including praying. And just like it was easier to copy a picture when you kept looking at the original, the more you keep your eyes on Jesus, the better you'll be able to follow His example.

How Jesus Prayed

We can see in the Bible how Jesus prayed. Read the following verses out loud, and then talk about what they have in common:

- Mark 1:35: "Early the next morning, Jesus woke and left the house while it was still dark. He went to a place to be alone and pray."

- Matthew 14:23: "After he said good-bye to them, he went alone up into the hills to pray. It was late, and Jesus was there alone."

- Luke 6:12: "At that time Jesus went off to a mountain to pray. He stayed there all night, praying to God."

Jesus loved to get away by Himself, late at night or early in the morning, and talk to His Father. It was during those times of prayer that God would give Jesus the strength He needed to carry out His mission on earth. If Jesus needed that strength from God, don't we need it too?

During the next few weeks, we will look at the different prayers that Jesus prayed. We will hear Him teach His disciples how to pray, and we will listen to His final prayers on the cross. Jesus was always talking to His Father . . . the *same* Father you can talk to any time of day or night.

Praying This Week:

Ask your mom or dad if you can get up a little bit earlier, or go to bed a little bit later, so that you can pray like Jesus often did—alone in a quiet place. Just thank Him, tell Him He is great, confess your sins to Him, and ask Him for His help. Then be still and listen. You will be following Jesus' example and making God's heart happy.

Jesus, thank You
for showing us
how great You are.
Help me to trust You.

Raising Lazarus

What is the biggest thing you have ever asked for? You might have asked for it from your parents, or maybe even from God. Did you receive what you asked for? Talk about that with your family.

Not Too Late

One of the prayers of Jesus is found in John 11. Mary and Martha were desperate for Jesus to do something very big for them. These two sisters followed Jesus and loved to serve Him and the disciples. They had a brother named Lazarus, and he became very sick. Since they had seen Jesus heal so many people from diseases, they wanted Him to come to their house and heal Lazarus. So they sent a message asking Him to come. Do you think Jesus came right away? No, He didn't! He actually waited *two more days* before starting His journey. By the time He arrived, Lazarus had been dead for four whole days. Mary, Martha, and all their friends were very sad, and they didn't understand why Jesus took so long to get there. It made Jesus sad to see His friends this way, and He cried.

But Jesus always has a reason for everything He does. At Lazarus's tomb He prayed, "'Father, I thank you that you heard me. I know that you always hear me. But I said these things because of the people here around me. I want them to believe that you sent me.' After Jesus said this, he cried out with a loud voice, 'Lazarus, come out!'" (John 11:41–43). And he did!

Trusting God's Plan

You see, Jesus' friends already knew that He could heal sickness, and Jesus wanted to show them something more. He wanted them to know that He had the power to bring Lazarus back to life!

Sometimes we might be sad because of bad things that happen in our lives. It's easy to think, *Jesus, why didn't You stop this from happening?* It's okay to ask that. But Jesus also wants you to trust Him. He wants you to remember that nothing that happens to you can mess up His plan and purpose for your life.

Praying This Week:

Is there anything in your life that you wish God would do something about? Is there anything big that you want Him to do, and you sometimes doubt that He will? Spend some time telling God that you trust Him. Ask Him for your "big thing," but then leave the result to Him. If He doesn't answer the way you want Him to, remember that God is *always* good and He *always* knows what's best for you!

Lord, please show me ways I can give You glory. Help me know how to do that and how to follow the example of Jesus.

The Glory of the Father

Think about the hardest or saddest thing you have ever been through in your life. Maybe you were sick, or you lost someone you love. Maybe you had some problems with friends or at school, or just had a very bad day. How did you handle that? Did you talk to others? Did you pray? Did you trust God? Were other people watching you? What did they see?

Jesus Prays Again

After Jesus raised Lazarus back to life, many people heard what had happened. They all wanted to find Jesus and follow Him. They wanted to see more of these miracles with their own eyes. This made some of the religious leaders angry, because they did not believe that Jesus was God's Son, and they thought He was making all of this up. When Jesus knew that they were coming after Him and that His journey to the cross was beginning, He turned to His Father. He didn't ask God to save Him from what was about to happen. Instead, He prayed, "'Father, bring glory to your name!' Then a voice came from heaven, 'I have brought glory to it, and I will do it again'" (John 12:28).

Glory to God

What is *glory*? What was Jesus asking God to do? *Glory* is something that makes you look great. It is when other people are amazed at you, and you are the one they are focused on. Giving God glory is telling people not to look at you but to look at God, since He is the one working in you! Giving God glory is making God famous—showing others that He is God and that He is the One who should be praised.

Jesus knew that even though He was about to suffer and die, the miracle of His resurrection from the dead would bring more glory to God's name than ever. And that was His heart's deepest desire, His prayer to His Father.

Praying This Week:

Do you ever have a hard time giving God glory? Do you sometimes want to keep some of it for yourself? We can learn a lot from this prayer of Jesus. If you are going through something hard this week, instead of asking God to take it away, pray that His name would become more famous because of you and your situation. Ask Him to let people see how you are trusting Him and how big and good He is. Now *that* is giving glory to your Father. And He deserves it!

Jesus, thank You for praying for me, for protecting me, and for making me one with You.

Jesus Prays for Me

Close your eyes and try to imagine this picture: Jesus is talking to His Father. He is praying for all of His friends and followers, and asking God to keep them safe from the evil one and to give them joy. Then He prays for someone else. Can you hear Him? He says your name. "Father, I pray for _____."
What would you guess He is praying for you?

Jesus' Prayer

In John 17, before Jesus went to the cross, He talked to His Father. He was thankful for His friends on earth, and He prayed for God to watch over them. Then He said this:

> I pray for these men. But I am also praying for all people who will believe in me because of the teaching of these men [that's you!]. Father, I pray that all people who believe in me can be one. You are in me and I am in you. I pray that these people can also be one in us, so that the world will believe that you sent me. . . . And the world will know that you loved these people the same as you loved me. (vv. 20–21, 23)

Being One

Jesus taught His disciples how to live. His disciples taught others, and, thanks to the Bible, God's Word, these things were passed down from generation to generation . . . all the way to us! The Bible you hold in your hand is there because people kept on passing down the things God had said. Even though it was thousands of years ago that Jesus was on earth, He knew you by name. He knew that one day you would choose to believe in Him and follow Him, and He had you in mind when He said this prayer.

He also knew that you would need help in this crazy world! He wanted you to be close to other people who follow Him so that you could all walk down this road together. That is what He means by "being one" with other people who believe in Him. He meant that we are all together, and that because we all love Him, we can all love each other.

So this is how Jesus asked His Father to help every-one who would ever be part of the family of God, including you. Can you believe that? Jesus—praying for *you*!

Jesus, Your
prayers on the
cross remind me
that You suffered,
and You did it
all for me.

Week 49

Prayers of the Cross

The time had come. Jesus had finished His ministry of teaching and healing, and now He would give His life as a sacrifice for us. He prayed that God would get the glory. He prayed for all of those who believed in Him and for those who would later believe. At the end of Jesus' life on earth, in all of His suffering, He prayed four prayers that we can learn from today.

- *Mark 14:36: "Abba, Father! You can do all things. Let me not have this cup of suffering. But do what you want, not what I want."* Jesus was asking God if there was any other way He could save the world from sin. He was saying, "Father, Daddy, please let there be another way!" Then He said something very important: "But do what You want to do, not what I want to do." He trusted that His Father knew best. And He obeyed.

- *Luke 23:34: "Father, forgive them. They don't know what they are doing."* Jesus was asking God to forgive the very people who

207

were putting nails in His hands, spitting on Him, and yelling mean things at Him. Even in all that pain and suffering, He was thinking about others and forgiving them.

- *Matthew 27:46: "My God, my God, why have you left me alone?"* You see, Jesus had all the sin of the world placed on Him. When God looked down at His Son, He could see every sin, every bad and dark thing that anyone had ever done or would ever do. God had to turn away, because a perfect, loving God cannot look at all that darkness. Jesus felt alone. He was longing to be with His Father again.

- *John 19:30: "He said, 'It is finished.' He bowed his head and died."* The whole reason Jesus had come to earth, the whole purpose of His being born in that stable and living a perfect life, had been completed. Jesus had suffered and died for us. His last prayer on the cross reminds us that it is finished . . . *forever.*

Praying This Week:

Think about the cross, and read over these prayers of Jesus. Tell Jesus that you trust His plan more than your own plan. Think about others, as He did, and thank Him for finishing the work of the cross so that you could be with Him forever.

Thank You, Lord,
for teaching us
how to pray!

The Lord's Prayer

One day Jesus was praying and some of His disciples were watching Him. When He was finished, they said, "Please teach us how to pray" (Luke 11:1). They knew it was important to talk to God, but they were not so sure about what to say. Jesus told them in Matthew 6:9–13:

> When you pray, you should pray like this: "Our Father in heaven, we pray that your name will always be kept holy. We pray that your kingdom will come. We pray that what you want will be done, here on earth as it is in heaven. Give us the food we need for each day. Forgive the sins we have done, just as we have forgiven those who did wrong to us. And do not cause us to be tested; but save us from the Evil One."

These verses are called the Lord's Prayer. You can pray the Lord's Prayer like this:

- **Our Father in heaven:** God, You are my Father! You are like a dad to me! You know me better than anyone else, and You are always watching over me. You are in heaven, and I am calling to You.

211

- **We pray that Your name will always be kept holy:** The name of Jesus is special. It is awesome! You are so good and right and clean and holy. I want to tell You how wonderful You are.

- **We pray that Your kingdom will come and that what You want will be done:** I know there are great things coming, Lord! And I want what You want. I pray that whatever You want to happen will happen.

- **Give us the food we need for each day:** We can always trust You to give us exactly what we need. Will You make sure we have everything we need? I know You will!

- **Forgive the sins we have done:** I have done many things that need forgiveness. Forgive me, Lord? And help me forgive those who have hurt me.

- **Do not cause us to be tested, but save us from the evil one:** Help me not to go near people or places that will make me want to do wrong. Watch over me and keep me safe.

Praying This Week:

Memorize the Lord's Prayer. Write it on a card or piece of paper, and keep reading it until you can say it by heart. Have your family say this prayer together before your meals this week. Once you have this memorized, you can begin using it as a pattern for your own prayers. Before long, you will be praying just like Jesus taught us to!

Thank You!
Wow!
I'm sorry!
Help!
I'm listening!

Putting It All Together

Have you ever learned a dance or something like a karate move? Show your family any kind of routine you have learned in the past. Most likely, you learned it one step at a time. Then you put all those steps together, and there it was!

Now that you have learned all about prayer, it's time to put it all together! Let's try it this way:

- **Thank You:** What can you thank God for today? Enter into His city with thanksgiving!

- **Wow:** What can you praise God for? What has He done? Why is He great?

- **I'm Sorry:** What do you need to confess today? He already knows, but just say it!

- **Help:** How do you need God's help? How do others need His help?

- **I'm Listening:** Don't forget to be still and listen! What is God saying to your heart?

Now that you understand why it is important to pray and exactly how to pray, one important ingredient is left . . . *just do it!* You see, praying is something we often want to do and know we need to do, but we get busy with other things. We think, *I will pray later.* Or, *I have to do this first.* God has taught you how to pray, so what will you do now? James 1:22–25 says,

> Do what God's teaching says; do not just listen and do nothing. When you only sit and listen, you are fooling yourselves. A person who hears God's teaching and does nothing is like a man looking in a mirror. He sees his face, then goes away and quickly forgets what he looked like. But the truly happy person is the one who carefully studies God's perfect law that makes people free. He continues to study it. He listens to God's teaching and does not forget what he heard. *Then he obeys what God's teaching says.* When he does this, it makes him happy.

Did those verses say that when we obey, God loves us more? No! It says that when we obey, we are helping ourselves! God loves us the same no matter what we do.

Praying This Week:

Use your prayer journal to focus on all the different types of prayers. Start with "Thank You" prayers the first day, "Wow" prayers the second, and so on. On the last day of the week, put them all together! Your prayers will be a beautiful sound to your Father's ears. He promises to listen.

Jesus, I'm glad I know
You better now! Thank
You for helping me
love You even more.

I'm Changed!

Let's test how well you know what your family looks like. Have everyone leave the room and secretly change one thing about how they look. It could be something they are wearing or the way they fixed their hair. Come back together, and try to guess the changes!

An Unchanging God

Did you know that God never changes? "Jesus Christ is the same yesterday, today, and forever" (Hebrews 13:8). Below are three things we know about God. Read this list, and look up the verses with your family:

- **God is omniscient**—This means that He knows everything! There is nothing He does not see or understand (Isaiah 46:9–10; Psalm 139:1–4).

- **God is omnipotent**—This means that He has all the power in the world! He is more powerful than anyone or anything. He can do *anything* (Matthew 19:26; Jeremiah 32:27).

- **God is omnipresent**—This means that He is everywhere all the time! No matter where you are, He's right there with you (Proverbs 15:3; Psalm 139:7–10). Wow!

God is so huge and mighty and powerful. He knows everything, He can do anything, and He is everywhere. Yet He wants to hear you talk to Him? What a cool thought! Prayer brings you closer to the heart of God, but it also does something to your heart. It changes you.

Your Changed Heart

Prayer doesn't change the way you look on the outside; it changes what you care about and the way you think about God. If you are thanking Him, you're more grateful for what you have. If you're praising Him, you are aware of what a great God you have. If you're saying, "I'm sorry" to Him, you are letting go of those sins that drag you down. If you are asking Him for help, you are reminding yourself that you can't do all of this alone! If you are listening to Him, you are hearing the God of the universe speak to you.

All of these things change you. They make you into a better person. They bring you closer to your God . . . all because of a prayer.

Praying This Week:

Spend some time writing in your prayer journal about the things you learned about prayer through this book. Do you know more now? Do you feel closer to Jesus? Talk about those things with your family. And as you go, remember the words of Paul in 1 Thessalonians 5:17: "Never stop praying"!

Learn to pray . . .
and learn the Bible!

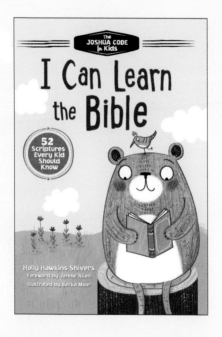

Learn 52 scriptures every kid should know in
I Can Learn the Bible.

For more information, visit www.tommynelson.com.